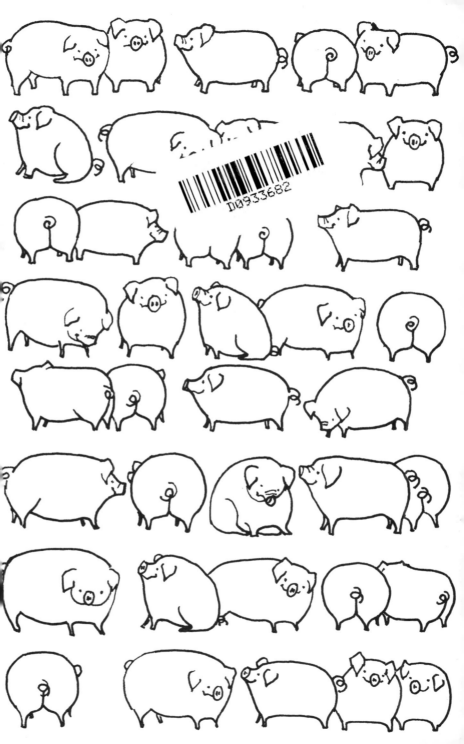

PIGMIES

IT'S A
PIG WORLD
OUT THERE

BY PHYLLIS DEMONG

PAUL S. ERIKSSON
Publisher
MIDDLEBURY, VERMONT

Printed in the United State of America.
987654321

Library of Congress Cataloging in Publication Data

Demong, Phyllis.
It's a pig world out there.
    1. American wit and humor, Pictorial. I. Title.
NC1429.D363A4   1980   741.5'973
79-6021   ISBN 0-8397-3989-3

CONTENTS

ACKNOWLEDGEMENTS

WITH PIG PEN AND OINCK
IN HAND IT BEHOOVES
THE AUTHOR TO GRUNT
CREDIT WHERE CREDIT
IS DUE · TO 'OINCKER' BERN-
STEIN · TO BETTY WHITE
(AMY'S MOTHER) TO JEAN
BOARADSHAW LYTTLE &
HER SON JEFF · TO SARAH
& TO JIM FREDERICKSON
FOR HIS TOOTH PIGS...
THANK YOU .

THE IMPORKANT ONES

U
HAM JØRDAN
IN THE WHITE SOWSE

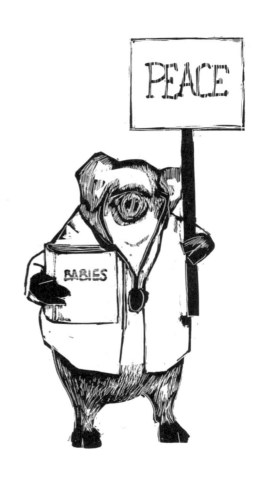

DOCTOR SPHOGK

LYDIA E. PIGHAM

CHAIRMAN OF THE BOARD
WITH PORKFOLIO

PIED PIPER OF HAMELIN

SHAMSON AND DELILAH

CUPIG

MARY PIGFORD

MOVING PIGTURE STAR

PIG BRACKEN

"I HATE TO SOWSKEEP…"

DOROTHY PORKER

EPIGSCOPALIANS

HAMLET

BY THE BOARD OF AVON

PORKTIA

FRANKENSWINE

LIZZIE BOARDEN

WITH AN AXE
HIT HER MOTHER 40 WHACKS...

WEARING CLHOGS

ULYSSES S.GRUNT

PORK RICHARD'S ALMANAC

CARY GRUNT

MOVING PIGTURE STAR

PIGGERTON DETECTIVE AGENCY

PIGASSO
PAINTING A PORKTRAIT

PIGASUS

GHAMBOLING ON THE BOARDWAI

BERT PORKS

CARL SANDBOARG

PIGGING OUT A TUNE

"THE HOG
COMES
ON LITTLE
CAT FEET"

SOWAGER EMPRESS

A PORKLY SOWAGER

THE GABOARS

GAY BOARS OUT OF THE CLOSET

MORE IMPORKANT ONES

JOHN SWINEBECK
JIM NABOARS
CAROL BOARNET
ERNEST HAMMINGWAY
LUCREZIA BOARGIA
PRINCESS PIGNATELLI
SOWDY DOODY
JOHN GRUNTHER
MONACHIM BACON

HOGARTH
MARY ROBERTS SWINEHART
RING LARDNER
GRAHAM GREEN
GRUNTLAND RICE
SEN. SOWARD BACON
GENE STRATTON PORKER
ED MC MAHAM
BILLY GRAHAM (BOARN AGAIN)

AND

BOARIS KARLOFF
HIPPORKRATES
PIGMALION
PIGLET (POOH'S FRIEND)
MISS PIGGY
ALEXANDER HAMILTON
SHAMUEL ADAMS
SHAMUEL THOMAS
SIR FRANCIS BACON
SWINEGALI
SHAM SPADE
REX SNOUT
DASHIELL HAMMET
DR. ZHIVHOGO
SEN. SHAM IRVIN
MR. PIGWICK
MARGARET PORK-WHITE
DICK VAN SWINE

GLORIA SWINESON

THE
SOWD OF MUSIC

PIGARO

THE BOARBER OF SEVILLE

SIR JOSEPH PORKER, K.C.B.

GILBOART AND SULLIVHAM

H.M.S. PIGAFORE

SWINE LAKE

BOARIS GODUNOV

GERSHWINE'S
PORKY AND BESS

BOARBERSHOP QUARTET

♪♪♪SINGING SWEET ADELSWINE ♪♪

PIGGY LEE

FRANK SWINEATRA

DAYS OF
SWINE AND ROSES

VICTOR BOARGE
PIGGING OUT A TUNE

KING OF SIHAM

SOWS PACIFIC

I WANNA HOLD YOUR HAM...

♪♪ SOME ENCHAMTED EVENING...

♪ RODGERS AND HAMMERSTEIN

♪ ♪ I GOT
RYTHAM......
COLE PORKER

YOU ARE MY SUNSWINE......

SWINE ON
SWINE ON
HARVEST MOON......

♩ ♫

SOWS OF THE BOARDER DOWN MEXICO WAY...

♪

AND

ROSES ARE BLOOMING IN PIGGARDY

MY FUNNY VALENSWINE	A. BOARODIN
PIG O' MY HEART	HAMDEL
SKARBOAROUGH FAIR	LANDSOWSKA
BOARN FREE	PIGGOLOS
SWINE-EE	ARPIGGIOS
SNOUT HEARTED MEN	GOOD DAY SUNSWINE

THE
WORLD OF
SPORKS

OLYMPIGS

SOWS PAW

THE CHAMP

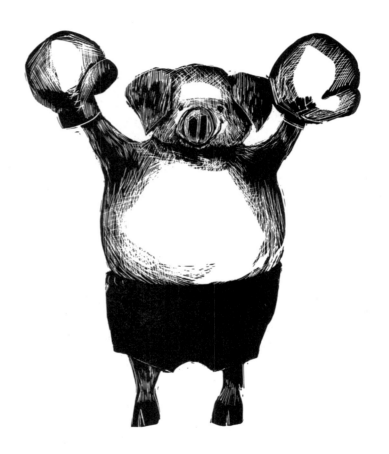

PIGNACIOUS!

GOOD SPORK!

BOBBY PIGGS
M.C.P.

JHOGGERS

DOROTHY HAMILL

PIGGY FLEMING

JUMPIG ROPE

HOGKEY PLAYERS

PORKAGE

ALSOW . . . .

MISCSOWLANEOUS

HAMPER

EMBOARDERY

HOW TO SOW A FINE SEAM

THE BAY OF PIGS

PIG LATIN
IG-PAY ATIN-LAY

PORK PIE

TAM-O-SHAMTER

HAMBOARG

BOARDELLO

BOY SNOUTS

GIRL SNOUTS

HAMMOCK

MIGRUNT
LABOARERS

SPIGOT

PIGOT

SOWSED

PIG-UP TRUCK

PIGTAIL

PIGGY BACK

SUPPORK HOSE

PIG-EON TOED

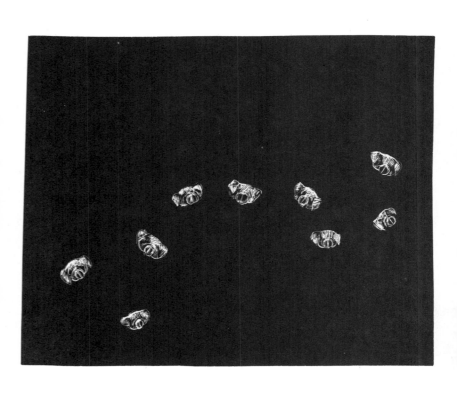

THE PIG DIPPER

SOW-WESTER

PORKNOGRAPHY

DISPIGABLE!

(NO PIG LEAF)

VAGRUNTS

PIG-POCKET

AND

PIGADOR
PRHOGNOSTICATIONS
SHAM
SHAMBLES
PIGSILATED
BOARED
SAND HOG
MUMBLETY-PIG
HOGSHEAD
WART HOG
PHOTHOGRAPHER
BOARN FREE

THE SOWD AND THE FURY
PIGGIN ENGLISH
PIGARESQUE
BOARN NAKED
BOARDOM
HAMMER
AURORA-BOAREALIS
PORK-MANTEAU
also..... WARTHOG
GROUND HOG
PORKUPINE
PIGTURE OF DORIAN GRAY

SONNETS FROM THE PORKUGUESE

PIG-UP-STICKS

GEHOGRAPHY

THE PIG TIME
BOARDWAY

JASON ROBOARDS
HAMMY GRIMES
SHAMMY DAVIS JR.
MARVIN HAMMISCH
JANE PIGGINS
HAMIONE GINGOLD
LIONEL HAMPTON
PIGMALION
MAJOR BOARBARA
CAT ON A HOG TIN ROOF
OINCKLE VANYA
SWINEY TODD
OAKLAHAMA

PORK AVENUE

THE PIG APPLE

NIEW HAMSTERDAM • GOTHAM •
PORK AUTHORITY • CENTRAL PORK
STATUE OF LIBOARTY • PORK OF ENTRY
SOWHO • BOARDWAY AND PORKY SECOND STREET

IMPORKS

WITH PASSPORKS

EXPORKS

TONGSUN PORK

SEAPORKS

NEWPORK RHODE ISLAND
PORKLAND MAINE
SAG HARBOAR NEW YORK
BAR HARBOAR MAINE
SHREVEPORK LOUISIANA
SHAM FRANCISCO CALIBOARNIA

IMMIGRUNTS

NO SPIGGA ENGLISH

DAVENPORK IOWA

CHICHOGO
HOG BUTCHER TO THE WORLD

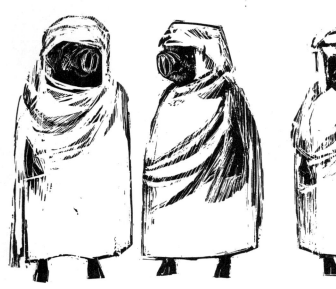

SOWDIES

SOWDI ARABIA

PIGGADILLY CIRCUS

DEPORKMENT OF INTERIOR

NATIONAL PORKS

OLYMPIG NATIONAL PORK
PIGHORN NATIONAL PORK
GRAND PORKAGE, MINN.
EL PORKAL NATIONAL PORK
YOSEMITE CALIBOARNIA

INTERNATIONAL BOARDERS

FROM HAMMOND'S ATLAS

WINNIPIG CANADA
SOWSKATCHEWAN CANADA
BACON GA.
SOWHEGAN ME.
CHAMBOARD QUEBEC
EASTHAM MASS.
CHAMPS ELYSEES (PARIS)
PORKUGAL
SOWETO
PORKSAID
PIGGSBURG PA.
BOOTHBAY HARBOAR ME.

PORK'S PEAK COL.
PORKEEPSIE N.Y.
HOG ISLAND N.C.
PORKLAND MAINE
BACON HILL (BOSTON)
LABOARDOR CANADA
WOODSTHOG VERMONT
PLACE PIGALLE (PARIS)
HAMSTERDAM HOLLAND
HAMILAYAS (TIBET)
BOARNEO
PORKNEY ISLANDS

BON APPIGTIF

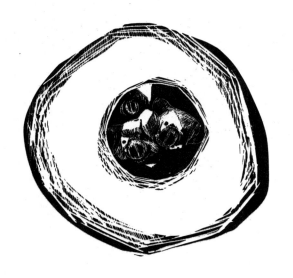

BAGELS AND HOGS

PIGNIC

PIGGALILLI

PIGGLED PIGS FEET

BOARDEAUX SWINE
FROM THE SOWS OF FRANCE

SPIGETTI

PIGEREL

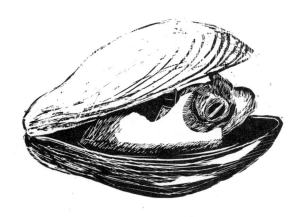

QUAHOG FOR CLHAM CHOWDER

WHISKEY SOWER

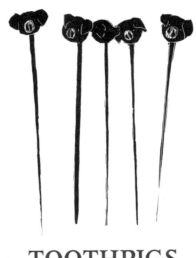

TOOTHPIGS

AND

PORKERHOUSE STEAK	PIG NEWTONS
GRHOG	PORK N' BEANS
GUINESS SNOUT	HAM N' EGGS
BOARSCH	HAM N' CHEESE
BOARSIN CHEESE	PIG KNUCKLES
SOWERKRAUT	PORKER HOUSE ROLLS
HAM BOARGERS	GRAHAM CRACKERS
CHOGOLATE MOUSSE	BACON SODA*

*MAY BE PURCHASED AT ALL PIGGLY WIGGLY STORES

OLD SOWS
&
CLICHÉS

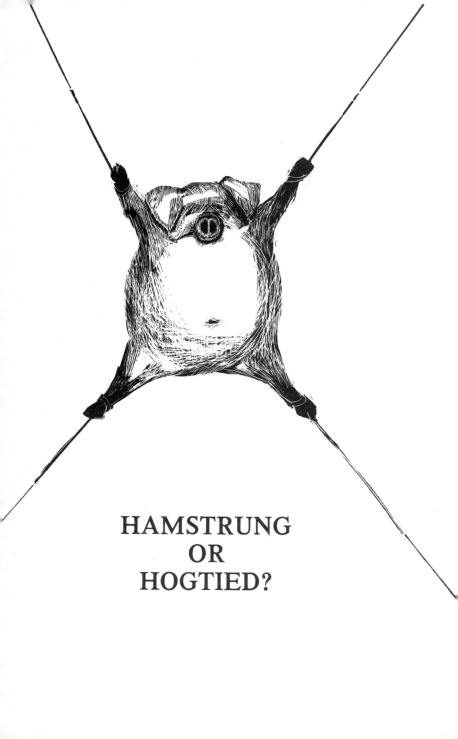

HAMSTRUNG
OR
HOGTIED?

"NEVER BUY A PIG IN A POKE"

FRAGRUNT
HOLLYHOGS

''PLEASE DON'T PIG THE DAISIES''

FLOWER BOARDER WITH PORKULACA

SOWER GRAPES

HOGWASH

"S'WINE YOU BE MY VALENTINE"

PORK BARREL

''IN A PIG'S EYE''

PRHOGNOSIS•PIGSTY

DO NOT PIG YOUR NOSE IN PUBLIC

HOG WILD
AND
HOPPIG MAD

AND

PIGAMENTS OF THE IMAGINATION
ASK NOT PORK WHOM THIS BELL TOLLS...
HIGGLETY PIGGLETY MY FAT HEN...
GO WHOLE HOG
HOGS AND KISSES
PORK QUOI? PORK QUOI PAS?
HOW NOW BROWN SOW?
IT'S SNOUT FOR ME TO SAY
HOG ON ICE
IT'S SNOUT OR NEVER
HAMMER AND TONGS
SOW'S TRICKS?
HORNSWHOGGLE
PIG DEAL!
GRUNT AND BEAR IT
TAKE FOR GRUNTED
MAKE A SILK PURSE FROM A SOW'S EAR
BRING HOME THE BACON
EAT HIGH OFF THE HOG
I THINK...THEREFORE I HAM
OUR SWINES HAVE TENDER GRAPES
AS IRISH AS PADDY'S PIG
TO MARKET TO MARKET TO BUY A FAT PIG...
THIS LITTLE PIGGY WENT TO MARKET...

EPIGLOGUE

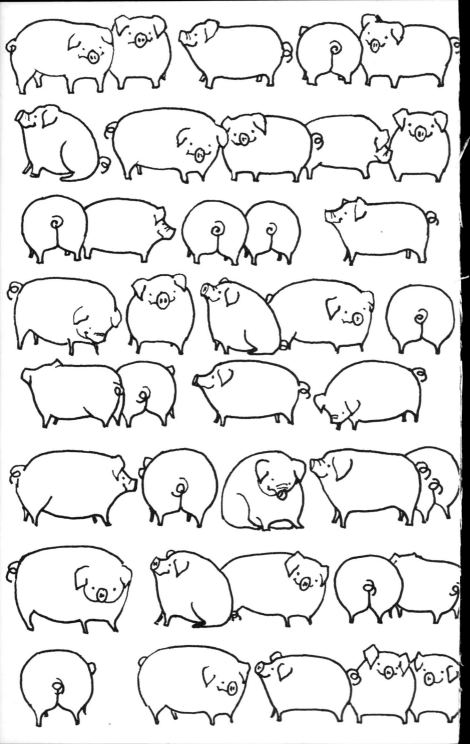